Soon To Be Mr. & Mrs.

Wedding Date:

Wedding Planner

WEDDING DATE & TIME:

VENUE ADDRESS:

BUDGET:

OFFICIANT:

WEDDING PARTY:

TO DO LIST:

NOTES & REMINDERS:

Wedding Budget Planner

	TOTAL COST:	DEPOSIT:	REMAINDER:
WEDDING VENUE			
RECEPTION VENUE			
FLORIST			
OFFICIANT			
CATERER			
WEDDING CAKE			
BRIDAL ATTIRE			
GROOM ATTIRE			
BRIDAL JEWELRY			
BRIDESMAID ATTIRE			
GROOMSMEN ATTIRE			
HAIR & MAKE UP			
PHOTOGRAPHER			
VIDEOGRAPHER			
DJ SERVICE/ENTERTAINMENT			
INVITATIONS			
TRANSPORTATION			
WEDDING PARTY GIFTS			
RENTALS			
HONEYMOON			

12 Months Before

- [ ] SET THE DATE
- [ ] SET YOUR BUDGET
- [ ] CHOOSE YOUR THEME
- [ ] ORGANIZE ENGAGEMENT PARTY
- [ ] RESEARCH VENUES
- [ ] BOOK A WEDDING PLANNER
- [ ] RESEARCH PHOTOGRAPHERS
- [ ] RESEARCH VIDEOGRAPHERS
- [ ] RESEARCH DJ'S/ENTERTAINMENT

- [ ] CONSIDER FLORISTS
- [ ] RESEARCH CATERERS
- [ ] DECIDE ON OFFICIANT
- [ ] CREATE INITIAL GUEST LIST
- [ ] CHOOSE WEDDING PARTY
- [ ] SHOP FOR WEDDING DRESS
- [ ] REGISTER WITH GIFT REGISTRY
- [ ] DISCUSS HONEYMOON IDEAS
- [ ] RESEARCH WEDDING RINGS

THINGS TO REMEMBER:

9 Months Before

- [ ] FINALIZE GUEST LIST
- [ ] ORDER INVITATIONS
- [ ] PLAN YOUR RECEPTION
- [ ] BOOK PHOTOGRAPHER
- [ ] BOOK VIDEOGRAPHER
- [ ] BOOK FLORIST
- [ ] BOOK DJ/ENTERTAINMENT
- [ ] BOOK CATERER
- [ ] CHOOSE WEDDING CAKE

- [ ] CHOOSE WEDDING GOWN
- [ ] ORDER BRIDESMAIDS DRESSES
- [ ] RESERVE TUXEDOS
- [ ] ARRANGE TRANSPORTATION
- [ ] BOOK WEDDING VENUE
- [ ] BOOK RECEPTION VENUE
- [ ] PLAN HONEYMOON
- [ ] BOOK OFFICIANT
- [ ] BOOK ROOMS FOR GUESTS

THINGS TO REMEMBER:

6 Months Before

- [ ] ORDER THANK YOU NOTES
- [ ] REVIEW RECEPTION DETAILS
- [ ] MAKE APPT FOR DRESS FITTING
- [ ] CONFIRM BRIDEMAIDS DRESSES
- [ ] GET MARRIAGE LICENSE
- [ ] BOOK HAIR/MAKE UP STYLIST
- [ ] CONFIRM MUSIC SELECTIONS
- [ ] PLAN BRIDAL SHOWER
- [ ] PLAN REHEARSAL
- [ ] SHOP FOR WEDDING RINGS

THINGS TO REMEMBER:

3 Months Before

- MAIL OUT INVITATIONS
- MEET WITH OFFICIANT
- BUY GIFTS FOR WEDDING PARTY
- BOOK FINAL GOWN FITTING
- BUY WEDDING BANDS
- PLAN YOUR HAIR STYLE
- PURCHASE SHOES/HEELS
- CONFIRM PASSPORTS ARE VALID

- FINALIZE RECEPTION MENU
- PLAN REHEARSAL DINNER
- CONFIRM ALL BOOKINGS
- APPLY FOR MARRIAGE LICENSE
- CONFIRM MUSIC SELECTIONS
- DRAFT WEDDING VOWS
- CHOOSE YOUR MC
- ARRANGE AIRPORT TRANSFER

THINGS TO REMEMBER:

1 Month Before

- CONFIRM FINAL GUEST COUNT
- CONFIRM RECEPTION DETAILS
- ATTEND FINAL GOWN FITTING
- CONFIRM PHOTOGRAPHER
- WRAP WEDDING PARTY GIFTS
- CREATE PHOTOGRAPHY SHOT LIST

- REHEARSE WEDDING VOWS
- BOOK MANI-PEDI
- CONFIRM WITH FLORIST
- CONFIRM VIDEOGRAPHER
- PICK UP BRIDEMAIDS DRESSES
- CREATE WEDDING SCHEDULE

THINGS TO REMEMBER:

1 Week Before

- FINALIZE SEATING PLANS
- MAKE PAYMENTS TO VENDORS
- PACK FOR HONEYMOON
- CONFIRM HOTEL RESERVATIONS
- GIVE SCHEDULE TO PARTY

- DELIVER LICENSE TO OFFICIANT
- CONFIRM WITH BAKERY
- PICK UP WEDDING DRESS
- PICK UP TUXEDOS
- GIVE MUSIC LIST TO DJ

THINGS TO REMEMBER:

1 Day Before

- GET MANICURE/PEDICURE
- ATTEND REHEARSAL DINNER
- GET A GOOD NIGHT'S SLEEP!
- GIVE GIFTS TO WEDDING PARTY
- FINALIZE PACKING

TO DO LIST:

The Big Day!

- GET HAIR & MAKE UP DONE
- HAVE A HEALTHY BREAKFAST
- ENJOY YOUR BIG DAY!
- MEET WITH BRIDESMAIDS
- GIVE RINGS TO BEST MAN

TO DO LIST:

Wedding Planner

ENGAGEMENT PARTY:

DATE: _____   LOCATION: _____

TIME: _____   NUMBER OF GUESTS: _____

NOTES:

BRIDAL SHOWER:

DATE: _____   LOCATION: _____

TIME: _____   NUMBER OF GUESTS: _____

NOTES:

STAG & DOE PARTY:

DATE: _____   LOCATION: _____

TIME: _____   NUMBER OF GUESTS: _____

NOTES:

Wedding Party

MAID/MATRON OF HONOR:

PHONE: DRESS SIZE: SHOE SIZE:

EMAIL:

BRIDESMAID:

PHONE: DRESS SIZE: SHOE SIZE:

EMAIL:

BRIDESMAID #2:

PHONE: DRESS SIZE: SHOE SIZE:

EMAIL:

BRIDESMAID #3:

PHONE: DRESS SIZE: SHOE SIZE:

EMAIL:

BRIDESMAID #4:

PHONE: DRESS SIZE: SHOE SIZE:

EMAIL:

NOTES:

Wedding Party

BEST MAN:

PHONE: _____ WAIST SIZE: _____ SHOE SIZE: _____

NECK SIZE: _____ SLEEVE SIZE: _____ JACKET SIZE: _____

EMAIL: _____

GROOMSMEN #1:

PHONE: _____ WAIST SIZE: _____ SHOE SIZE: _____

NECK SIZE: _____ SLEEVE SIZE: _____ JACKET SIZE: _____

EMAIL: _____

GROOMSMEN #2:

PHONE: _____ WAIST SIZE: _____ SHOE SIZE: _____

NECK SIZE: _____ SLEEVE SIZE: _____ JACKET SIZE: _____

EMAIL: _____

GROOMSMEN #3:

PHONE: _____ WAIST SIZE: _____ SHOE SIZE: _____

NECK SIZE: _____ SLEEVE SIZE: _____ JACKET SIZE: _____

EMAIL: _____

GROOMSMEN #4:

PHONE: _____ WAIST SIZE: _____ SHOE SIZE: _____

NECK SIZE: _____ SLEEVE SIZE: _____ JACKET SIZE: _____

EMAIL: _____

Photographer

PHOTOGRAPHER:

PHONE: _____   COMPANY: _____

EMAIL: _____   ADDRESS: _____

WEDDING PACKAGE OVERVIEW:

EST PRICE: _____

INCLUSIONS:	YES ✓	NO ✓	COST:
ENGAGEMENT SHOOT:			
PHOTO ALBUMS:			
FRAMES:			
PROOFS INCLUDED:			
NEGATIVES INCLUDED:			

TOTAL COST: _____

Videographer

VIDEOGRAPHER:

PHONE: _____ COMPANY: _____

EMAIL: _____ ADDRESS: _____

WEDDING PACKAGE OVERVIEW:

EST PRICE: _____

INCLUSIONS:	YES ✓	NO ✓	COST:
DUPLICATES/COPIES:	☐	☐	
PHOTO MONTAGE:	☐	☐	
MUSIC ADDED:	☐	☐	
EDITING:	☐	☐	

TOTAL COST: _____

NOTES:

DJ/Entertainment

DJ/LIVE BAND/ENTERTAINMENT:

PHONE: _____ COMPANY: _____

EMAIL: _____ ADDRESS: _____

START TIME: _____ END TIME: _____

ENTERTAINMENT SERVICE OVERVIEW:

EST PRICE: _____

INCLUSIONS:	YES ✓	NO ✓	COST:
SOUND EQUIPMENT:			_____
LIGHTING:			_____
SPECIAL EFFECTS:			_____
GRATUITIES			_____

TOTAL COST: _____

NOTES:

Florist

FLORIST:

PHONE: _____ COMPANY: _____

EMAIL: _____ ADDRESS: _____

FLORAL PACKAGE:

EST PRICE: _____

INCLUSIONS: YES ✓ NO ✓ COST:

BRIDAL BOUQUET: ☐ ☐ _____

THROW AWAY BOUQUET: ☐ ☐ _____

CORSAGES: ☐ ☐ _____

CEREMONY FLOWERS ☐ ☐ _____

CENTERPIECES ☐ ☐ _____

CAKE TOPPER ☐ ☐ _____

BOUTONNIERE ☐ ☐ _____

TOTAL COST:

Wedding Cake/Baker

PHONE: _____ COMPANY: _____

EMAIL: _____ ADDRESS: _____

WEDDING CAKE PACKAGE:

COST: _____ FREE TASTING: _____ DELIVERY FEE: _____

FLAVOR: _____

FILLING: _____

SIZE: _____

SHAPE: _____

COLOR: _____

EXTRAS: _____

TOTAL COST: _____

NOTES: _____

Transportation Planner

TO CEREMONY: PICK UP TIME: PICK UP LOCATION:

BRIDE:

GROOM:

BRIDE'S PARENTS:

GROOM'S PARENTS:

BRIDESMAIDS:

GROOMSMEN:

NOTES:

TO RECEPTION: PICK UP TIME: PICK UP LOCATION:

BRIDE & GROOM:

BRIDE'S PARENTS:

GROOM'S PARENTS:

BRIDESMAIDS:

GROOMSMEN:

Wedding Planner

BACHELORETTE PARTY:

DATE: _____   LOCATION: _____

TIME: _____   NUMBER OF GUESTS: _____

NOTES:

BACHELOR PARTY:

DATE: _____   LOCATION: _____

TIME: _____   NUMBER OF GUESTS: _____

NOTES:

CEREMONY REHEARSAL:

DATE: _____   LOCATION: _____

TIME: _____   NUMBER OF GUESTS: _____

NOTES:

Wedding Planner

REHEARSAL DINNER:

DATE: _____	LOCATION: _____

TIME: _____	NUMBER OF GUESTS: _____

NOTES:

RECEPTION:

DATE: _____	LOCATION: _____

TIME: _____	NUMBER OF GUESTS: _____

NOTES:

REMINDERS:

_____

_____

_____

_____

_____

Names & Addresses

CEREMONY:

PHONE: _____   CONTACT NAME: _____

EMAIL: _____   ADDRESS: _____

RECEPTION:

PHONE: _____   CONTACT NAME: _____

EMAIL: _____   ADDRESS: _____

OFFICIANT:

PHONE: _____   CONTACT NAME: _____

EMAIL: _____   ADDRESS: _____

WEDDING PLANNER:

PHONE: _____   CONTACT NAME: _____

EMAIL: _____   ADDRESS: _____

CATERER:

PHONE: _____   CONTACT NAME: _____

EMAIL: _____   ADDRESS: _____

FLORIST:

PHONE: _____   CONTACT NAME: _____

EMAIL: _____   ADDRESS: _____

Names & Addresses

BAKERY:

PHONE: _____ CONTACT NAME: _____

EMAIL: _____ ADDRESS: _____

BRIDAL SHOP:

PHONE: _____ CONTACT NAME: _____

EMAIL: _____ ADDRESS: _____

PHOTOGRAPHER:

PHONE: _____ CONTACT NAME: _____

EMAIL: _____ ADDRESS: _____

VIDEOGRAPHER:

PHONE: _____ CONTACT NAME: _____

EMAIL: _____ ADDRESS: _____

DJ/ENTERTAINMENT:

PHONE: _____ CONTACT NAME: _____

EMAIL: _____ ADDRESS: _____

HAIR/NAIL SALON:

PHONE: _____ CONTACT NAME: _____

EMAIL: _____ ADDRESS: _____

Names & Addresses

MAKE UP ARTIST:

PHONE: _____ CONTACT NAME: _____

EMAIL: _____ ADDRESS: _____

RENTALS:

PHONE: _____ CONTACT NAME: _____

EMAIL: _____ ADDRESS: _____

HONEYMOON RESORT/HOTEL:

PHONE: _____ CONTACT NAME: _____

EMAIL: _____ ADDRESS: _____

TRANSPORTATION SERVICE:

PHONE: _____ CONTACT NAME: _____

EMAIL: _____ ADDRESS: _____

NOTES:

Caterer Details

CONTACT INFORMATION:

PHONE: _____   CONTACT NAME: _____

EMAIL: _____   ADDRESS: _____

MENU CHOICE #1:

MENU CHOICE #2:

	YES ✓	NO ✓	COST:
BAR INCLUDED:	☐	☐	_____
CORKAGE FEE:	☐	☐	_____
HORS D'OEUVRES:	☐	☐	_____
TAXES INCLUDED:	☐	☐	_____
GRATUITIES INCLUDED:	☐	☐	_____

Menu Planner

HORS D'OEUVRES

1st COURSE:

2nd COURSE:

3rd COURSE:

4th COURSE:

DESSERT:

1 Week Before

	THINGS TO DO:	NOTES:
MONDAY		
TUESDAY		
WEDNESDAY		
THURSDAY		

REMINDERS & NOTES:

1 Week Before

	THINGS TO DO:	NOTES:
FRIDAY		
SATURDAY		
SUNDAY		

LEFT TO DO:

REMINDERS: NOTES:

Wedding Guest List

NAME:	ADDRESS:	# IN PARTY:	RSVP: ✓

Wedding Guest List

NAME:	ADDRESS:	# IN PARTY:	RSVP: ✓

Wedding Guest List

NAME:	ADDRESS:	# IN PARTY:	RSVP: ✓

Wedding Guest List

NAME:	ADDRESS:	# IN PARTY:	RSVP: ✓

Wedding Guest List

NAME:	ADDRESS:	# IN PARTY:	RSVP: ✓

Wedding Guest List

NAME:	ADDRESS:	# IN PARTY:	RSVP: ✓

Wedding Guest List

NAME:	ADDRESS:	# IN PARTY:	RSVP: ✓

Wedding Guest List

NAME:	ADDRESS:	# IN PARTY:	RSVP: ✓

Wedding Guest List

NAME:	ADDRESS:	# IN PARTY:	RSVP: ✓

Wedding Guest List

NAME:	ADDRESS:	# IN PARTY:	RSVP: ✓

Wedding Guest List

NAME:	ADDRESS:	# IN PARTY:	RSVP: ✓

Wedding Guest List

NAME:	ADDRESS:	# IN PARTY:	RSVP: ✓

Wedding Guest List

NAME:	ADDRESS:	# IN PARTY:	RSVP: ✓

Wedding Guest List

NAME:	ADDRESS:	# IN PARTY:	RSVP: ✓

Wedding Guest List

NAME:	ADDRESS:	# IN PARTY:	RSVP: ✓

Wedding Guest List

NAME:	ADDRESS:	# IN PARTY:	RSVP: ✓

Wedding Guest List

NAME:	ADDRESS:	# IN PARTY:	RSVP: ✓

Wedding Guest List

NAME:	ADDRESS:	# IN PARTY:	RSVP: ✓

Wedding Guest List

NAME:	ADDRESS:	# IN PARTY:	RSVP: ✓

Wedding Guest List

NAME:	ADDRESS:	# IN PARTY:	RSVP: ✓

Wedding Guest List

NAME:	ADDRESS:	# IN PARTY:	RSVP: ✓

Wedding Guest List

NAME:	ADDRESS:	# IN PARTY:	RSVP: ✓

Wedding Guest List

NAME:	ADDRESS:	# IN PARTY:	RSVP: ✓

Wedding Guest List

NAME:	ADDRESS:	# IN PARTY:	RSVP: ✓

Wedding Guest List

NAME:	ADDRESS:	# IN PARTY:	RSVP: ✓

Wedding Guest List

NAME:	ADDRESS:	# IN PARTY:	RSVP: ✓

Wedding Guest List

NAME:	ADDRESS:	# IN PARTY:	RSVP: ✓

Wedding Guest List

NAME:	ADDRESS:	# IN PARTY:	RSVP: ✓

Wedding Guest List

NAME:	ADDRESS:	# IN PARTY:	RSVP: ✓

Wedding Guest List

NAME:	ADDRESS:	# IN PARTY:	RSVP: ✓

Wedding Guest List

NAME:	ADDRESS:	# IN PARTY:	RSVP: ✓

Wedding Guest List

NAME:	ADDRESS:	# IN PARTY:	RSVP: ✓

Wedding Guest List

NAME:	ADDRESS:	# IN PARTY:	RSVP: ✓

Wedding Guest List

NAME:	ADDRESS:	# IN PARTY:	RSVP: ✓

Wedding Guest List

NAME:	ADDRESS:	# IN PARTY:	RSVP: ✓

Wedding Guest List

NAME:	ADDRESS:	# IN PARTY:	RSVP: ✓

Wedding Guest List

NAME:	ADDRESS:	# IN PARTY:	RSVP: ✓

Wedding Guest List

NAME:	ADDRESS:	# IN PARTY:	RSVP: ✓

Wedding Guest List

NAME:	ADDRESS:	# IN PARTY:	RSVP: ✓

Wedding Guest List

NAME:	ADDRESS:	# IN PARTY:	RSVP: ✓

Wedding Guest List

NAME:	ADDRESS:	# IN PARTY:	RSVP: ✓

Wedding Guest List

NAME:	ADDRESS:	# IN PARTY:	RSVP: ✓

Wedding Guest List

NAME:	ADDRESS:	# IN PARTY:	RSVP: ✓

Wedding Guest List

NAME:	ADDRESS:	# IN PARTY:	RSVP: ✓

Wedding Guest List

NAME:	ADDRESS:	# IN PARTY:	RSVP: ✓

Wedding Guest List

NAME:	ADDRESS:	# IN PARTY:	RSVP: ✓

Wedding Guest List

NAME:	ADDRESS:	# IN PARTY:	RSVP: ✓

Wedding Guest List

NAME:	ADDRESS:	# IN PARTY:	RSVP: ✓

Wedding Guest List

NAME:	ADDRESS:	# IN PARTY:	RSVP: ✓

Wedding Guest List

NAME:	ADDRESS:	# IN PARTY:	RSVP: ✓

Wedding Guest List

NAME:	ADDRESS:	# IN PARTY:	RSVP: ✓

Wedding Guest List

NAME:	ADDRESS:	# IN PARTY:	RSVP: ✓

Wedding Guest List

NAME:	ADDRESS:	# IN PARTY:	RSVP: ✓

Wedding Guest List

NAME:	ADDRESS:	# IN PARTY:	RSVP: ✓

Wedding Guest List

NAME:	ADDRESS:	# IN PARTY:	RSVP: ✓

Wedding Guest List

NAME:	ADDRESS:	# IN PARTY:	RSVP: ✓

Wedding Guest List

NAME:	ADDRESS:	# IN PARTY:	RSVP: ✓

Wedding Guest List

NAME:	ADDRESS:	# IN PARTY:	RSVP: ✓

Wedding Guest List

NAME:	ADDRESS:	# IN PARTY:	RSVP: ✓

Seating Chart Planner

Table #

Table #

Table #

Table #

SEATING PLANNER NOTES:

Seating Chart Planner

Table #

Table #

Table #

Table #

SEATING PLANNER NOTES:

Seating Chart Planner

Table #

Table #

Table #

Table #

SEATING PLANNER NOTES:

Seating Chart Planner

Table #

Table #

Table #

Table #

SEATING PLANNER NOTES:

Seating Chart Planner

Table #

Table #

Table #

Table #

SEATING PLANNER NOTES:

Seating Chart Planner

Table #

Table #

Table #

Table #

SEATING PLANNER NOTES:

Seating Chart Planner

Table #

Table #

Table #

Table #

SEATING PLANNER NOTES:

Seating Chart Planner

Table #

Table #

Table #

Table #

SEATING PLANNER NOTES:

Seating Chart Planner

Table #

Table #

Table #

Table #

SEATING PLANNER NOTES:

Seating Chart Planner

Table #

Table #

Table #

Table #

SEATING PLANNER NOTES:

Seating Chart Planner

Table #

Table #

Table #

Table #

SEATING PLANNER NOTES:

Seating Chart Planner

Table #

Table #

Table #

Table #

SEATING PLANNER NOTES:

Seating Chart Planner

Table #

Table #

Table #

Table #

SEATING PLANNER NOTES:

Seating Chart Planner

Table #

Table #

Table #

Table #

SEATING PLANNER NOTES:

Seating Chart Planner

Table #

Table #

Table #

Table #

SEATING PLANNER NOTES:

Seating Chart Planner

Table #

Table #

Table #

Table #

SEATING PLANNER NOTES:

Seating Chart Planner

Table #

Table #

Table #

Table #

SEATING PLANNER NOTES:

Seating Chart Planner

Table #

Table #

Table #

Table #

SEATING PLANNER NOTES:

Seating Chart Planner

Table #

Table #

Table #

Table #

SEATING PLANNER NOTES:

Seating Chart Planner

Table #

Table #

Table #

Table #

SEATING PLANNER NOTES:

Seating Chart Planner

Table #

Table #

Table #

Table #

SEATING PLANNER NOTES:

Seating Chart Planner

Table #

Table #

Table #

Table #

SEATING PLANNER NOTES:

Seating Chart Planner

Table #

Table #

Table #

Table #

SEATING PLANNER NOTES:

Seating Chart Planner

Table #

Table #

Table #

Table #

SEATING PLANNER NOTES:

Seating Chart Planner

Table #

Table #

Table #

Table #

SEATING PLANNER NOTES:

Seating Chart Planner

Table #

Table #

Table #

Table #

SEATING PLANNER NOTES:

Seating Chart Planner

Table #

Table #

Table #

Table #

SEATING PLANNER NOTES:

Seating Chart Planner

Table #

Table #

Table #

Table #

SEATING PLANNER NOTES:

Seating Chart Planner

Table #

Table #

Table #

Table #

SEATING PLANNER NOTES:

Seating Chart Planner

Table #

Table #

Table #

Table #

SEATING PLANNER NOTES:

Seating Chart Planner

Table #

Table #

Table #

Table #

SEATING PLANNER NOTES:

Seating Chart Planner

Table #

Table #

Table #

Table #

SEATING PLANNER NOTES:

Seating Chart Planner

Table #

Table #

Table #

Table #

SEATING PLANNER NOTES:

Seating Chart Planner

Table #

Table #

Table #

Table #

SEATING PLANNER NOTES:

Seating Chart Planner

Table #

Table #

Table #

Table #

SEATING PLANNER NOTES:

Seating Chart Planner

Table #

Table #

Table #

Table #

SEATING PLANNER NOTES:

Seating Chart Planner

Table #

Table #

Table #

Table #

SEATING PLANNER NOTES:

Seating Chart Planner

Table #

Table #

Table #

Table #

SEATING PLANNER NOTES:

Seating Chart Planner

Table #

Table #

Table #

Table #

SEATING PLANNER NOTES:

Seating Chart Planner

Table #

Table #

Table #

Table #

SEATING PLANNER NOTES:

Seating Chart Planner

Table #

Table #

Table #

Table #

SEATING PLANNER NOTES:

Seating Chart Planner

Table #

Table #

Table #

Table #

SEATING PLANNER NOTES:

Seating Chart Planner

Table #

Table #

Table #

Table #

SEATING PLANNER NOTES:

Seating Chart Planner

Table #

Table #

Table #

Table #

SEATING PLANNER NOTES:

Seating Chart Planner

Table #

Table #

Table #

Table #

SEATING PLANNER NOTES:

Seating Chart Planner

Table #

Table #

Table #

Table #

SEATING PLANNER NOTES:

Seating Chart Planner

Table #

Table #

Table #

Table #

SEATING PLANNER NOTES:

Seating Chart Planner

Table #

Table #

Table #

Table #

SEATING PLANNER NOTES:

Seating Chart Planner

Table #

Table #

Table #

Table #

SEATING PLANNER NOTES:

Seating Chart Planner

Table #

Table #

Table #

Table #

SEATING PLANNER NOTES:

Seating Chart Planner

Table #

Table #

Table #

Table #

SEATING PLANNER NOTES:

Seating Chart Planner

Table #

Table #

Table #

Table #

SEATING PLANNER NOTES:

Seating Chart Planner

Table #

Table #

Table #

Table #

SEATING PLANNER NOTES:

Seating Chart Planner

Table #

Table #

Table #

Table #

SEATING PLANNER NOTES:

Seating Chart Planner

Table #

Table #

Table #

Table #

SEATING PLANNER NOTES:

Seating Chart Planner

Table #

Table #

Table #

Table #

SEATING PLANNER NOTES:

Seating Chart Planner

Table #

Table #

Table #

Table #

SEATING PLANNER NOTES:

Seating Chart Planner

Table #

Table #

Table #

Table #

SEATING PLANNER NOTES:

Seating Chart Planner

Table #

Table #

Table #

Table #

SEATING PLANNER NOTES:

Seating Chart Planner

Table #

Table #

Table #

Table #

SEATING PLANNER NOTES:

Seating Chart Planner

Table #

Table #

Table #

Table #

SEATING PLANNER NOTES:

Made in the USA
Columbia, SC
04 January 2020